I Have a Family

Rachel Coe • Illustrated by **Don Fields**

Broadman Press
Nashville, Tennessee

© Copyright 1987 • Broadman Press
All rights reserved
4241-72

ISBN: 0-8054-4172-7
Library of Congress Catalog Card Number: 86-17629
Dewey Decimal Classification: C306.8
Subject Heading; FAMILY

Printed in the United States of America

Library of Congress Cataloging-in-Publication Data

Coe, Rachel, 1952-
  I have a family.

  (Bible-and-me)
  1. Family—Religious life—Juvenile literature.
2. Children—Religious life. I. Fields, Don.
II. Title. III. Series.
BV4526.2.C6 1987   248.4   86-17629
ISBN 0-8054-4172-7

To

My children, who give me endless joy,
My husband, who loves and leads me
My mother, who encourages me,
        and
My father, whose memory lives within me.

My name is Dan.
I am three years old.

I live in this house with my family.

My mommy is in my family.

My mommy says, "I love you, Dan."

Mommy and I like to cook.
I use her wooden spoons and big bowls.

I stir, stir, stir.

My daddy is in my family.
My daddy says, "I love you, Dan."

My daddy likes to run. Running is fun! I like to run, too. I get tired. Then Daddy carries me on his shoulders.

At night, Daddy helps me get my toothbrush.

Then Daddy tells me a Bible story. I like to look at the pictures in my Bible.

I have a brother. His name is Matt. He is ten
years old. He is bigger than I am.

Matt and I are buddies. He likes to draw
pictures. I like to draw, too. Matt lets me use his
paper and crayons.

I draw a picture of a boat.

Matt says, "Good, Dan! That's pretty!"

I have another brother. His name is Marc.
He's seven. He's bigger than I am, too.

Marc and I play ball. Marc says, "Run, Dan. Get the ball." Marc tries to catch me! I run and laugh!

I have five people in my family—
  My mommy, my daddy
    my brother Matt, my brother Marc, and me!

My family goes to church.
I like my room at church.
Daddy lets me knock on the door.

My family goes on picnics. We eat hot dogs. We drink cold lemonade. Yum, Yum!

My family takes walks.

Sometimes we look for pretty rocks.

My family goes on trips.

One time we went to a zoo.

Everyone in my family likes ice cream!

We eat together. Daddy prays, "Thank You, God, for our food. Thank You, God, for our family."

Sometimes I say thank you to God.

God gave me a family.
My mommy loves me.
My daddy loves me.
Matt and Marc love me.
And Mommy and Daddy tell me God loves me, too!